You Can't Buy a Dinosaur with a Dime

Problem-Solving in Dollars and Cents

Harriet Ziefert
pictures by Amanda Haley

🍎 Blue Apple Books

To my mom
—A.H.

Text copyright ©2003 by Harriet Ziefert

Illustrations copyright ©2003 by Amanda Haley

All rights reserved. CIP Data is available.

First published in the United States 2003 by

🍎 Blue Apple Books

515 Valley Street, Maplewood, NJ 07040

www.blueapplebooks.com

First published in paperback by Blue Apple Books 2007

Printed in the USA 04/17

ISBN: 978-1-60905-146-4

Pete has nickels, quarters, dimes—
He'd like to buy a toy.
If he can pay for what he wants,
he'll be a happy boy.

Mom says, "Pete, the money's yours
to spend at Harry's Store,
And if you choose to spend it all,
then you can save some more."

Pete finds a scary dinosaur,
as green as sour pickles.
He Wonders how much it will cost
in quarters, dimes and nickels.

Pete lines all his quarters up,
    and then adds seven dimes.
Unsure of the total sum,
    he counts it two more times.

Pete's bank is almost empty now.
He puts it on a shelf.
He has a brand-new dinosaur
and thirty cents total wealth.

Pete holds Tyrannosaurus Rex.
He names him Ugly Jack.
Then he reads a comic book,
"If Dinosaurs Came Back!"

At dinner Pete is looking sad.
He wishes for more money.
Though he likes his dinosaur,
an emptied bank feels funny.

"You'll get two dollars," says his dad,
"if you clean the yard.
Then you can start to save again.
The work is not too hard."

Pete carries out old papers...

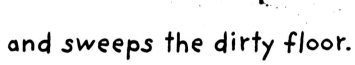

and sweeps the dirty floor.

He sorts through the recycling
and puts it by the door.

"Here are eight new quarters,"
his dad says with a smile.
Pete is glad to get them—
he'll save them for awhile.

When Pete gets his allowance,
he puts it in his bank.

Five dimes and five nickels—
clinkity, clinkity, clank!

.75 (allowance)
2.00 (Yard clean-up)
+ .30 (change at store)
_____
$3.05

How much is your allowance?

Lucky Pete! He finds a dime
on his way to school.

Pete puts the money in his bank—
six nickels and a dime.
Forty cents goes through the slot,
one coin at a time.

Pete hears the car keys jingling.
Dad's walking out the door.
"I'd like to come along," Pete says,
"to shop at Harry's Store."

Can you count out
coins equal to
the amount of money
Pete has?

The store is full of pretty things
all lined up row by row.
But Pete is after dinosaurs
and knows just where to go.

A small dino costs two dollars.
A triceratops is three.
Pete says, "The little dinosaur
is a better price for me."

Pete makes a tough decision.
Dad's waiting at the door.
He chooses Stegasaurus—
and won't spend any more.

Pete carries his own package.
Dad says, "Let's get a snack.
And you can bank your money
as soon as we get back."

Money Fun

Get to know your coins by doing rubbings of the front and back of each coin.

Put a coin underneath a piece of paper and rub lightly with a pencil until the image comes through, just like this:

According to a survey made by the magazine Zillions: Consumer Reports for Kids, about half the kids received a regular weekly allowance. The typical allowance for 9- and 10-year-olds is $3.00.

Do your own survey. Talk to 6 kids you know. What do they receive in allowance? Show your results on a chart.

	50¢	75¢	$1.00	$1.50
Emma				
Nate				
John				
Will				
Jill				

Ways to earn money:
    Bringing in mail or newspapers, cat feeding, dog walking, leaf raking, lawn watering, weeding, snow shoveling, helping at birthday party.
    Which job would you like to do?
    Make a job-wanted poster to let people know you are available.

Did you ever buy something because it looked good to you in a store or on a TV commercial, then were disappointed with your purchase? Nearly everyone has had such an experience.
    What was yours? Tell about it in a letter to your mom or dad.

Give to charity.
    One thing you can do with money you earn is to give some of it away to people in need or to causes you believe in.
    What will you do this year? And if you can't give money, perhaps you would like to volunteer and donate your time.

Facts About Money

1 The first clearly recorded use of marked coins was by the Greeks just after 700 B.C. Before pieces of metal were used (copper, bronze, iron, gold and silver), many things were tried out: seeds, cowrie shells, stones, leather, animal teeth, beads, salt, corn, feathers, grain.

2 Today all the coins we use are produced in one of four government mints. All the bills we use are printed at the U.S. Bureau of Engraving and Printing in Washington, D.C.

3 The tiny letter to the right of the face on the dime is called the mint mark. It tells you where the coin was minted:

D is for Denver
O is for New Orleans
P is for Philadelphia
S is for San Francisco

P is for Philadelphia

4 At one time or another, we have had a twenty-cent coin, a half-cent coin, a two-cent coin, and even a three-cent coin. The Lincoln penny that we use today was first issued in 1909 to mark the 100th anniversary of President Abraham Lincoln's birth.

5 It is the law that any picture of American money cannot be printed its actual size. It must be printed either bigger, or smaller, than it really is.

6 Counterfeiters rarely bother to make fake coins. They usually make fake bills and all governments try to make it very difficult to copy their paper money. That's why most counterfeit money is easily spotted.

7 The name "piggy bank" comes from a kind of clay called "pygg." Money stored at home in jars made of this clay came to be called pygg banks. Eventually, people began making them in the shape of pigs and the name changed to piggy bank.

8 Words for money:

  dough, moolah, gelt, cash,
  two bits (quarter),
  four bits (fifty cents),
  greenbacks (bills), bucks,
  quid (a pound sterling)

9 Expressions we use:

"penny-pincher"—a person who does not like to spend
"two cents worth"—a person who must always give an opinion
"a penny for your thoughts"—what someone says when he
        wants to know what you're thinking
"a plugged nickel"—something worthless
"nickel and diming"—bargaining and being cheap
"your bottom dollar"—the lowest price
"you look like a million bucks"—you look great